The Switch Yards

poems by

Michael Rerick

Finishing Line Press
Georgetown, Kentucky

The Switch Yards

ACKNOWLEDGMENTS

Sections of this book appear in similar form at the following gracious journals:
Cab/Net, Cue, Diagram, No Tell Motel, Order+Decorum, and *Word for/Word.*

These folks helped shape this manuscript: All family, Stephanie Balzer, Andy
Breuninger, Sommer Browning, Ann Fine, Lois Kemp, Melissa Koosmann, Tony
Mancus, Kristi Maxwell, Susanna Mishler, Lisa Morgan, Christian Peet, Dawn
Pendergast, Keri Oldham, Portland, Michael A. Rerick, Morgan Lucas Schuldt,
Joann and Oscar Swanson, The MFA program at UA, Tucson, and everyone I
missed. And, of course, Finishing Line Press' Christen Kinkaid, Kevin Mains,
Leah Mains, and everyone at the press. Thank you!

Publisher: Leah Maines

Editor: Christen Kincaid

Cover Art: © 2017 Keri Oldham / Artists Rights Society (ARS), New York

Author Photo: Michael Rerick

Cover Design: Elizabeth Maines McCleavy

Printed in the USA on acid-free paper.
Order online: www.finishinglinepress.com
          also available on amazon.com

Author inquiries and mail orders:
Finishing Line Press
P. O. Box 1626
Georgetown, Kentucky 40324
U. S. A.

Table of Contents

The Switch Yards

Light and light twists escalate

a sudden synaesthesia

in a tense buzz of birds

peeping the bathroom window,
how many birds, how many
others—it's early, coffee almost—
harmonizing

collected

each morning

and each morning

                              a walk

                    of ten miles
          in   the sand storm dream,   in the morning
                ten miles to sleep,   a dream   of animals
                    in violent love,   in the morning
                            in the same bed,
          ten miles   and the science of building a myth
          detection machine   dream,
                    in the morning, dusting sand
                    from the sheets,   a walk of ten
          thousand thousand miles to make love
          and sleep

and dream the

     shipping clerk sings:

     "Every ship hull, exterior,
     exterior, load torqued, floats
     in its skin of land, land
     ho! contents pressed heavy,
     contents and bilge."

     To which the crane man replies:

     "The slap trap of waves
     and gulls diving and fish
     darting, high here I am
     above, a loose skin

lifting metal cargo crates."

When they were younger, (hurried) notes. Worries

(away) during visits—   not all parts of the body connect
the miles a thing stretches before it rests.   And older,   this name
          part of the many names for this place:

architecture toggles between
architecture. In the musical
sense, circa 1374, the featherless
can't snatch light from the windows
or the windows. Concrete grows
faux boulders and foam over
the approach of heat, barricade
and disperse heat in the space
between two architectures making space.
In the cool gap, a convection agent
disables bird after bird into the road.
Shuttle, shuttle, circa 1338, of sun
peeks behind the clouds and fills
this ecstasy bath like a famous statue

or parts of a statue
packed in straw
to a light sonata of

matter mechanics (the sun reacts in its nuclear way) producing symboligies, but gone—crap left behind, the empty ledge, plant pieces back in their place—this does not show a pre-cat sleep-twitch or a lizard: a mosquito is what a mosquito is. A hand opens and closes in this manner, surprised by the picture of a place never been to, given by a friend from that place, a college campus

where parts of air
move in tight shorts,
another in a silk poncho—
tarps orange tarps blue loose
from the hot dog and soda cart
speak into the groans of the library,
the gym, through the squirrel chatter—
and the impish wind tosses along
the sidewalk under the berry tree
in open cages for birds, experiments,
birdseed, seed; a sweep of anxious
detectives blur the peripheral eye clean
to warm human approaches;
the inner narrative plays again—
each sentence across the lawn begins
"I am..." followed by
this percentage of man
this percentage of woman
found in the inside of TV,
the little hum, the absence of gears—
the honest parts of pants fall
over legs, buttons float over chests,
these hinged to a head: each part

                              takes in and moves out, rubs
                              against the neck to speak or hear

the mutiny before the mutineer
each Thursday in a romance cycle
of card games: shuffle shuffle. Thrust
and parry, the king and queen play
over apostrophes, dangle so
one pimps suits into pieces
the other sets on the board
of Odysseus' bed game

it's flat
                          raised and strong
leaves in the weave of the blanket
                          no space
a marker
                          a marker
what's
                          feathers, more feathers
why always the couch
                          move
later

Thursdays, they come in coats,

leave in drunk cartographer coats singing to the topography:

I photograph you smoking
with wine drinking soldiers
and blasts of surrendered minutia music
of defeated soldiers conquering then defeated
in the photograph of you
united in your clothes
hundreds marching through the background
not the knot of your skin too tight to undo
I spy
your ear chew music and wine
injects to enact the crumpled negative of
a surrender sword handed over
so borders flank in the zoom lens
but you push through and blur
and wine surrenders and mixes and ferments
your bright skin a blend so smooth I cannot catch the difference
surrounded by dead defeated soldiers
and you smoking
with risen conquering soldiers in the background
smoking
the mirror of wine molecules
while defeated soldiers untie your clothes but not the knot of your skin
not the knot of your skin
flanked by a conquered background
smoking defeated soldiers
smoking your surrounded borders

to wine music
so borders flank with the zoom lens but you push through and blur
smoking the photograph I took of you smoking spies
as I photograph you smoking.

The legend key reads
part future part night.
Voices recorded, dirt-
generations of map
makers and maps
the map makers make,
catalogued and stored:

We speculate Marvin's. What "grocery" and "store" mean. Marvin—no one names their child Marvin anymore—flies his goods in by helicopter. One day it's crates of toothpaste, another banana boxes. The helicopters remind us of birds, the flats strung under and swinging, eggs. We've heard of modernity nests here. Marvin's shrewd. We never see him but the picture, like the picture of a bust, hung above the customer service booth. We speculate his mysticism because all these mysteries. It's up to us, then, to explain the store's arrangement according to color rather than product.

Detergent next to oranges. Our children working there—which makes them Marvin's children too—cannot explain the bulk bins of beef and beets; and in turn, they turn against us in the usual way. When pressed, they say: this is the way it is. When we were children we played in the swamp Marvin's used to be. We fill our cars in the parking lot on days the helicopters come. On the 2nd of each month ten birds fly in and lay their eggs. Some are calculating—late into the night—the number of miles each water bottle travels. A Saturday tea group maps and charts where our things go. We repeat the slogan in blue under the red Marvin's sign: "where we are now." It was a joke. If someone stubbed their toe, we would say "where we are now." Now we do not laugh. Some have begun to say Marvin is a visionary.

                                        Rolled for tube transport, a map
                                        folded without creases, circles in
                                                                    circles

adopted and translated: sheets of adaptation screens

            produced by the iodine machine (hauled in, locked down)

                            stinking of its roving green light.

            Off Mylar
            bluelines
            spring pixels of
            brain hardware
            into eyes
            prompting landscapes
            of visible air
            between
            romance and war.

Later, "I walk better, but can't go fast." Circa the bicycle wheel, elite recovery clothes, fitting-in, clubs. That is, the Anti-Catharsis Calisthenics Movement provides both strength and beauty in its militants. The Movement's leader (beautiful leader) wears magnet strings that make trees kiss, bushes scherzo. Flyers and listservs exert pressure through seclusion: inclusion (as leader teaches) will lead to solidarity.

Behind a magnetic field's action
balance and heat take place:
heaven and decent jobs,
reserved for intolerant angels.
Warnings
blink across the cafeteria,
a sudden notion of what it's like   to be eaten
held, buffeted   by a magnetic pillow.

A wave
of medical terminology describes the moon:
"as university appointed social workers, we cannot understand why
the poor don't talk more
of money and religion."

After the great disaster
the hazard team claims:
worm-free water, cured cancer,
fixed ghettos.

Security articles
defer to the textbook

Proper Bush Names To Hide In: A Survey Of Surveillance

(public libraries catalogue *lost*) purports, best
camouflage lies in leaves (diagramed in numerology
and order). States: plant close to home, fodder
with found stuffed animals. Admits open bushes
work when proper contortions are performed
(illustrated in the appendix). High ranked bushologists
achieve the ability to mimic memory sounds
(chapter 4). The introduction cautions: some bushes
eject those hidden, make useless. Boxed first editions
(out of print, though photocopies, incomplete, exist)
sit in school yards moved over seas, always over
the next sea. Those who know nothing of the art have seen
bushes. Masters in palm fronds twist into a lion eating
an alligator (embossed on the cover). An essay explicates:
commoners can sense being surveyed by rolling back their eyes
and standing like

a bird

in cosmic spectra announces an inaudible noise,
                    occurrence, called spiral colliding
                    dual galactic gamma emissions: how
                    far they have traveled to be introduced—
                    through circles and triangles—through
                    wars, in wars: to name burst a singular
                    surrounded by plural, seen from singular,
                    song of plural, day shifting tense with night
                    though both a singular day: the post runs
                    or at least the handling and carrying
                    and getting of, carries the irrefutable
                    billboard of the anguished man alone
                    in a field under emissions shed faster
                    and faster away, jokes and arguments over
                    needs: a solid totem, a pocket of smoke:
                    One: the moon is a marshmallow pillow;
                    Two: the moon is a cold bitch;
                    Three: the moon is hard and floats.

And.

The music box plays ha ha again,
ants working strings on strings
in there. But the music box inserts
encyclopedic people measuring
time. What's the history, population,
and location of a name in Arabic,
in Latin? Bible? And next to the bible
the dictionary—why a dictionary
and encyclopedia are two different
books. Or, they are not. Page corners
categorical, bookmarked with notes
written in place of complete thoughts.

Or.

Moments, and between moments, stars, the freckled kind along the arm
or scattered in the dip where the spine floats. A clover of words spread.
Smells lucky from tiny pieces of velvet, flowers, buzz under trees
that feel the wind. A cat comes over in the concrete world, not expanding
itself, but with everything else.

And.

Everywhere the lyric knight
      story begins a warm day with marigolds invisible in the marigold
sun. The hero ruffles the paper: the morning and a cold bowl of bananas.
Thinks: this is another war, and blacks paragraphs with a felt marker. All
over the day: it's that choir again! Later, the knight sits in an electric car
and thinks: I will drive till all flowers turn red. The news informs with
information all down the street.

In a bunch of trees, smooth near the spider webs. At a corner a little nervous
and shorter than the knight. Outside the fancy restaurant so clean, shiny.
And the museum, a reminder and postcard.

Reluctant but finally won over by film. It's the kissing, and every actor
employs one, at least. Kiss after kiss the device: no one watching kisses.
But, when the actors sit, they all sit.

I have an empty chest, and others add, of drawers? Using super glue all the
mirrors get glued together, but the seventh, leaning in a corner. When the
parents visit they sit on the couch and drink very real lemonade. This is
very good, they say.

The knight eavesdrops on alcohol friends and etymology tales. One, the
hero sleeps on the floor; another, dancing on a fifty-foot window ledge; yet
another, jumps from the roof and slits the neck.

The bicycle purchase day: perfect, two wheels. The hero chisels a rock, a
helmet. What is more skull than a thing once liquid, what we walk on?
Seven bread loaves packed, the knight sets off, pointing a rolled *Scientific
American* at the nearest mountain line. A woman walking her dog hears
the shout.

At a hostel the knight brings a case of beer and a carton of cigarettes. This
is called the mediation of the great hall.

In a moonless desert, O, loneliest of nights, stars sparkling in the bicycle's chrome frame. A plane rumble creeps into the camp's little glow. O, night! The mumbling sound barrier says, Lyric Knight! Fumbling into rock, waving the magazine: plane! With base: you buy your way into things, you purchase the gold of things, this land will be paid for. Plane! The jet wings, winks a green light and moves away.

Page 79: *the big bang did not explode, but expanded everywhere, all the time; not in any noticeable way.*

This body heat fits, the hero considers, peddling the street grid under awnings to steady and blinking people: warm, soft people so obvious in their skin. But maple tree-ogres, pansy bed-vampires, lurk. The knight jumps and the yellow and purple lair flares! Ten,

then twenty, slain in a swoop (petals sticking to the lips). A rush to the closest with its tall, spreading fingers.

And of the many heroes another

in this small room or all rooms in one
where a candle flares with sparks
and an unexpected drift of almond
as strange as a hat or underwear
in a drawer never seen before, and
the cat's tail brushing the flame
will catch the bookshelf on fire
but lo, it does not, so experiments
with olive oil, paint thinner, hairspray,
and gasoline, but nothing will burn
the books from the bookshelf, and
someone switched the window glass
and carpet, so careful walks, then
stomps and though the floor holds
the carpet shakes loose a little
and the candle cannot burn that either,
so try the door handle but the sink
turns on and laughter and laughter
somewhere, but seriously, a problem,
so stiffen the pillow, and dig through
the ceiling, but the neighbors expect this
and too much barbed wire and rifle fire
to get through, so try the refrigerator,
but after months, nothing discovered
but the other always walking beside
who looks like ice cream and laughter
and laughter but things are getting
serious, and what flies flies out

a flush of pushpins to puncture heart valves via words through air (dramatic and only).

Outside, tetherball. A simple complex compound, a ball tethered to a tether tethered to the pole tethered to concrete tethered to the ground tethered to mass tethered to force. A game with ball and chain or rope for twisting, a parameter of collision, the skill of rebuttal and counter-rebuttal. Insert children, insert a school. Surround with a) houses b) trees c) desert. A simple structure necessary—no matter how far hands evolve from the head. Slack in the line between anchor and ball before the strike, slack remains a residual in bed, at work, traveling along the axis of vacation

or business, business or pleasure, business class or coach, nature of business, none of your, no personal relations in place of business, a business not a charity, small vs. big, open for business

a long cruise within the border of nation to visit
national monuments, natural monuments on post-
cards like billboards of the strange, traveling around
the far glow of city in nothing-stretches hiding house
distances where top and bottom lock into masculine
and feminine contours, a foreign country wrapped
in a familiar language

"hello, howdy, how ya'll doin, alright."

In this topography

of minute inertia exists

a bull raining golden showers of swans   finding open places
to fall into, circa 1900: "so much depends" on a steel mill for a soup can;
the bomb sprouts in flowers, the horses and people (the bodies slip
away);
an octopus reinvented through the many cracks of water is followed
by a melting bird in a palm;   an etherized metro   in a city
              seen from   an airplane or mountain car
       collects the air   and at night dances with twinkles
recorded in so many *Log of Dead Birds: a Symbology of Concrete*
       lining magazine racks.

                         .
                    the dirty job of distribution

a tune
the dishwasher sings to the dishes:
not yet not yet, yet
not yet not yet not yet,
yet
not yet not yet, yet,
yet

all holidays

over plates, glasses: chip temptation (the tiny squares of windshield after an
accident) so tempting the cupboard's full

a thumb pressed over the garden hose
a thumb swollen stiff
along the marvelous slick eucalyptus tree bark

                              Going home alone can never happen again,
                              so many in the beginnings,

                                                  hello my name is
                                                  hello my name is

and any combination of the two, synaptic
along the neural pathway to feed,
talk to the cat, say, cat, all optical on the table,
paw prints on the paper:

Dr. M. interprets the language
of domestic tabbies,
though other domestic languages
cannot be cracked.

The saucer glows and hums behind Footless Mary
floating down the ramp. Awestruck observers
slip deeper in the mud for the weight of this vision.

Along the Lock shore
Mr. D. and the watery head
of a large monster
cruise at a collision's pace.

"I cannot forget the smell
of brimstone," notes a woman
skilled with her feet, born w/o arms.

Light-years reunion a moment
from the fringe of two walking the park,
a frightening mechanism
of replay, holding hands

                                        from the beginning
fingers (small enough to be   two places
                          at once)
conduct, rise together from the body source
one hand, or two of two, walks, hears

                              "I am featherless, ha ha, I am featherless"

away from one code,

far into another:

Fast forward (FF>>): 1948 adaptation to the O.E. adverb (simply) "swiftly," not waiting. Finger and toe extensions push and orchestrate musical and movie copies and rentals. Commissioned public projects consist of clever and nonrelated pieces. >> re-reproduced; see catalogue.

Sendmail from the world (British Eng. sense of *forwards* taking "a definite direction" more than any other possible direction): Forward (Fwd); as opposed to O.E. archaic linear "toward the front" circa 1596 and Amer. Eng. in all senses but *forwards*.

N. device: Rewind (<<REW). 1717 editorial usage continues, though acts of going back and/or doing over remain reserved for leisurists, those that cannot help but see more clearly, they purport. See forward.

Far from home Reply (Re). Cannot "turn back" (O.Fr.), "back again" or "fold back" but give, give. Got what you sent, here it is back. An echo.

Into the trap, Play (Play >). Which n., play-by-play, depends on the v., frolic. Considered both unrestrained (knowing you are alone in a foreign country) and within parameters (institution experts and mass rates).

Compose (Compose) v. for organized quiet, later dispute, later interpret, later "on the record," later did you get my letter?

Yes.

                    So marriage, packing
in the desert, the slow car trip through reinventions of
        gorge, bridge, waterfall,   snow
sights of miniature monuments,   peripheral movements,

            conflicting reports over the radio:

[a race for the object. they
            found the tiny sculpture of a woman. we are waiting for them
        to find the woman.

it grabbed my leg, and when i yelled, it wriggled off to the trees.

we maintained an objective distance, but something went wrong.
chance. intimate
contact and communication.

it was disappointing,
all pale and dead by the time we got there.

our ships debilitate their machines.
investigation
        involves extracting engines from their hard bodies.

what looked like a child came up.

many similarities.
thin skin.
optics.

through the trees it looked like the sun setting a bonfire.
coming to, i was stiff in the neck where the scar is.

behavior exhibited in their internal transmitters
confounds us:
two bags for intake and exhaust
multiple lobes,

some inefficient but active
minor organs
leaking cells.

our organization tells the truth. they are
real, like us.

wind. mosquitoes. holidays.
we're blamed for everything.

i was on a table with something hard, cold going up my nose. but i couldn't
see what
        pushed it.

forced intercourse. and, often, tolerable
                                children are
produced.

like anyone, but for the eyes.
it came in the bedroom window
the first time. and the other times i can't remember.

concerning control, they hate to lose it.
wait. they despise waiting.

i hate i missed it.
three shallow imprints around a circle of burnt grass
                                like a big camp stove
                        turned upside down.

we assemble our ships round and soft, swiftly,
they imitate.]

(Past the billboard of the anguished man beginning his first trip
in three dimensions. To find melting snow. He collects
brown, hollow plant stems, red straws, and limp cardboard.
He secrets the bundles for years and binds them with twine.
In the Season the Streets Fill with Water, the trees swell
and drip. He launches and drifts out, away from the lights.)

(The black screen sways flat and deep, fields of trees, shadow,
and wind. The anguished man does what feels like gliding
through a representation of panorama, what only changes
with what must be the effect of glide or appears to be glide.
In part of a representation of an hour, the shadow parts
turn a slight gray. From here the sky becomes a little apparent.
He removes mortar and pestle from his coat using hands,
for it's too dim for his eyes. Breaking a small bit from the sky
he grinds it to powder. This takes the time it takes to represent
the change in another form of an hour, so all the gray
disappears. In the sound of what must be a form of wind,
he spreads the powder over what must be a thing for eating.
The part of darkness that extends, extends.)

"Back home" and "remember when" fall away, potent
decision making ingredients:

snap

or snavel,
      reunderstood as this particular today that does not stand
to stand. The queen invented (trees on the move), chess reinvented,
the question where move moves from, goes,
fits into (spaces like hair vibrate "mate"). Applying snappy
(gravity) to the sense-map:

Land
here in
this
that spot
where

all at the tree house
they lift the pears up

Watching from the house through the colding window, action:

                                        outside they skate,

all over and react

                        to tickets:

                "Skateboarding is Not a Crime" stuck everywhere.

Always an eye for urban landscape structures:

                                        stairs, handrails, loading docks,

                        security guards.

The pleasure of tricks

                loud: objective and precise.

Movie after movie portrays it wrong.

Movie goers memorize lines. Gaps

evolve. Sophisticated adaptations:

                                                the chipper
                                sounds like   smoke and leaves
(not the panda
joke)

                        the panda smells   of smoke
and leaves   no,   the chipper

                          the panda smokes and chokes,   leaves
                 the
                 chipper
                 joke
                 smokes

      the panda joke(s),

(s)mokes, leaves   chips

the   sound   of jokes   leave pandas in
             leaves   of   smoke
      every chipper every joke every panda smokes leaves to every   sound

      s m o k e l i k e

                          no joke,

                                                        the smoking
panda sounds
      like leaves,
leaves chipper

          the chipper smells   and sounds

the panda joke   sounds

like smoking

l
e
a
v
e
s

through   a   chipper
                                    the panda

                                    jokes

and

                                                            leaves

Book adaptations get it wrong.

Science conditions mass
audiences to understand
complicated theories,

    though the audience mistrusts
    unleashing, being the layman.

    "We now know so much."
    "We now know so much."

The last turns from the lectern.

The last's eye twitches.

A pocketbook of superstitions:

<u>Lightning:</u>

Does strike twice.

Stowed mirrors and scissors attract counting so
open doors and windows
                              (westerly hill triangulated against backyardly walnut)
             to seconds stepping mile by mile—
when it settles next to the couch,   don't,
                                   looking attracts the strike
        i.e. *Look, your uncle took a gun to himself. His son saw. Who's mad, now?*
as trees know. Knotty peepers.

                              Last June hit with hatchet shaped stones,
                              arrow head lightning stones,
                              Last June hit with flashes.

            Look up,
       and during storms,
            away.

The Empire State Building gets hit sixty-eight times every three years.

                         Never burn what was burnt by lightning:
live in silk sheets and feather pillows,
i.e. *He shot up the house, too. The owner says the ceiling cannot be*
       patched-up.
                         click your tongue into the mattress three times
       for the Virgin makes lightning,
                         a place-hold for His coming,
time to cross against goat hooves.   Three thank yous.

Wind from cumulus clouds pushes planes down
       i.e. *He never flew. He never went much of anywhere. Either of them.*
like a sneeze and it's over.

A chant *against* love: "May lightning crush you…"

For love, slip mirrors into the hair: "Come away from the hawthorn…"

> In temperate climates
> the air grows cold and dark.
> Children evacuate pools.
> In warmer climates storms
> come on so quick tourists
> spend hours in bars.

> > The Mongolian Hordes wore silk. When arrowheads struck, they
> > extracted easily. The metal knights felled and fell.

Never point it out
    i.e. *Thunder, to this day, scares the shit out of me.*
to others—a surety not even rubber will insulate.

               Some say some attract more
because there is something hard and cold inside.

Cutlery:

Pile ordinary utensils, silver scoop on top of tine—
criss blades in every cross combination
in the kitchen, hardwood full of small holes,
some bread knives stuck and strumming
tiny swivel notes, make religion by picking up
after another, desire the waiting for another to look, desire
to drop, desire sound. Cook beans and stir the pot
with knives. Enter slow witted as the devil, clumsy
with affection, the kitchen—steeped in gas, let the beans
boil over. Enter like a baby. Wait with breasts
bent inward. Climb through the wood avoiding stainless steel
like sharp clamps and handleless scalpels; near misses scrap clean
as a hole in the heel, sawed open to get the splinter—
just crawl. Rearrange the knives and drop them,
light jagged over the entrance. Split the beans, fire
glances and drool at another's feet, grow down to an infant,
be am, be gone, be am, never wonder where.
Enter in polite conversation about beans. Leave the gas on
the empty pot, gas filling the kitchen, filling the kitchen,
water everywhere, enter and drop the crosses, religion of falling,
knives with hardwood to sink into. Devil wood,
slow in crawling into the heel. Breasts as bags of beans,
love, beans with other beans, falling and picking each other up
in the bag on the chest. Enter, wait, and drop a knife.
Enter and play the bread knives, enter
and leave ordinary, crawling over wood, sprout eating sprout,
babies with sharp teeth, rearranging here, gone,
where; then in the next room with little scars.

The last from the lectern turns.

The white man goes home. He feels manly characteristics, says: "I'm oppressed whitely." Does not react. Says: "I am not a rebel, there is no rebellion against me." Political, he points differences into a corner, says: "stay."

"We're happy to report the war on (something) begins."
"We're happy to report the war on (something) is over."

Throughout the city individuals
become surprised by metal
working against metal to sound
what sounds like animal,

casting calls.

The sorority play begins with a table

> Krista, hands spread: "This morning bums me"
> "Yes" Missy near the table, legs apart
> "My parents," Linsi adjusts her skirt, "monsters,
> vacationing"

The light alternates between smoky and a wash
The audience enters the intense emotion under words, paused body parts, muscle
flicks
The spectacular wardrobe is spare
Behind a complex assemblage of colloquialisms, the audience sympathizes
Before the curtain slowly flutters down under a ΠΠΠ banner:

> "You are my sisters? You are my sisters"

The white man thinks harmonious   (he thinks)
        with everything:
possible resolutions   (world peace)

        on television:

        "Sucka," and "fool," and
        "pity." Mr. T wears green,
        looks B.A., smuggles guns
        and grins. He flies in.
        Mr. T learned to fly.
        He describes his house
        in a wealthy suburb,
        says he likes the chainsaw
        sound through the trees,
        the view this gives the neighbors.
        "Sucka," "fool."
        Mr. T explains his cartoon self
        and the sidekick: he heard
        a dog slammed in a door
        somewhere in the distance.
        He likes kids,
        loves kids. "Sucka," he says.
        "Fool, listen…"
        and his voice fades
        under machinegun rattle.

The white man thinks

        Mr. T protects his

                    children,

        at windows watch
        the train approach. The town descends.

Ticket lines form because the hidden thing
reveals itself. Men watch men tunnel through the earth
or play the piano with their feet. Women watch women
undress multiple breast tattoos. Children fight to inherit
the industrial empire. If they decide to go home. The city
contracts a walkway in the shape of a snake after all
the trees wither. If they decide to stay. The three-headed dog
personality trait behind chicken wire. Flap after flap they enter
the warm interior, which, through many embroideries, feels
like the many doors of home. Outside they wait with money
in hand. Among them, a dangerous absence of clowns.

Walking from the river, before the casino, the fingers of a woman

                         practice prelude maneuvers
through an air bow over violin strings
                                        silvered
                                        with pluck strides,
                 carrying lightning through a wash,
screeches of flood, melodies
                    across a serrated desert
                                        through a conifer grove:
born two feet
        up, falling, dead
born two feet
        up, falling, dead
as fifteen feet high
                flower, nut, leaf,
                    one by one the hairs fly loose
in a reformation of the fingers
                    she's between Glen Gould and Bach,

                    out with their recording career
                    with other stars. Gone copper, gone gold
                    in darkness, all directions a dim planet away,
                    the performance sounds like

EXPLANATION OF RECORDING COVER DIAGRAM

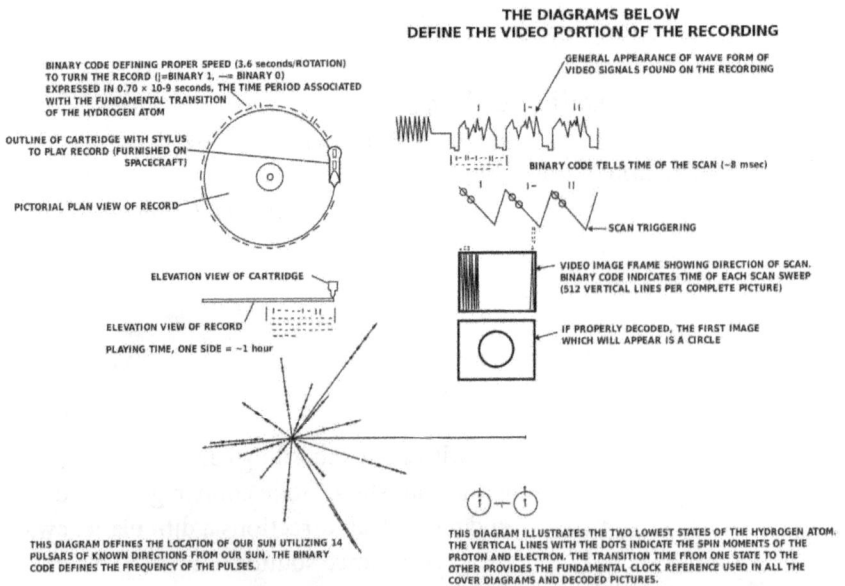

**THE DIAGRAMS BELOW
DEFINE THE VIDEO PORTION OF THE RECORDING**

BINARY CODE DEFINING PROPER SPEED (3.6 seconds/ROTATION)
TO TURN THE RECORD (|=BINARY 1, — BINARY 0)
EXPRESSED IN 0.70 × 10-9 seconds, THE TIME PERIOD ASSOCIATED
WITH THE FUNDAMENTAL TRANSITION
OF THE HYDROGEN ATOM

OUTLINE OF CARTRIDGE WITH STYLUS
TO PLAY RECORD (FURNISHED ON
SPACECRAFT)

PICTORIAL PLAN VIEW OF RECORD

ELEVATION VIEW OF CARTRIDGE

ELEVATION VIEW OF RECORD

PLAYING TIME, ONE SIDE ≈ ~1 hour

GENERAL APPEARANCE OF WAVE FORM OF
VIDEO SIGNALS FOUND ON THE RECORDING

BINARY CODE TELLS TIME OF THE SCAN (~8 msec)

SCAN TRIGGERING

VIDEO IMAGE FRAME SHOWING DIRECTION OF SCAN.
BINARY CODE INDICATES TIME OF EACH SCAN SWEEP
(512 VERTICAL LINES PER COMPLETE PICTURE)

IF PROPERLY DECODED, THE FIRST IMAGE
WHICH WILL APPEAR IS A CIRCLE

THIS DIAGRAM DEFINES THE LOCATION OF OUR SUN UTILIZING 14
PULSARS OF KNOWN DIRECTIONS FROM OUR SUN. THE BINARY
CODE DEFINES THE FREQUENCY OF THE PULSES.

THIS DIAGRAM ILLUSTRATES THE TWO LOWEST STATES OF THE HYDROGEN ATOM.
THE VERTICAL LINES WITH THE DOTS INDICATE THE SPIN MOMENTS OF THE
PROTON AND ELECTRON. THE TRANSITION TIME FROM ONE STATE TO THE
OTHER PROVIDES THE FUNDAMENTAL CLOCK REFERENCE USED IN ALL THE
COVER DIAGRAMS AND DECODED PICTURES.

wrapped in aluminum, whale hellos.

                              The river and cards shuffle her feet.

The river deals the alfalfa farmer cows and pigs,
the river falls away, sings,
                        from city
across ocean to city, of sea cows and kelp beds,
beds of grain raised for fish
                        "to eat, to eat."

                    While actions everyday perform
                    potential
                              projects,   though   not
                    always   fit for a project,

a host of sparrows leave a sparrow behind to re-sing the clamor
of day pitch by pitch

and something simple and human walks amazed
through electrons through photons
called light,
all possible,

and amazed to see the street
erode slowly away,
the shift from white to monochromatic another see, street,
but still the simple human amazed at the sound of a sparrow sounding like many.

In the eastside

of any city

the masoned church opens its thick doors
Sundays, certain saint days, charitable on hinges, secretive with locks;
inside candles and arched ceilings hum, outside
the eastside says "How long must I noun before you?" as a thin coat of rain
changes the color of the ground.

       Not far off, the cemetery spreads. Drizzle in the
maple, oak, and pine, over names wearing less and less of
themselves.

A documentary runs matinee:

Three CEOs.
        "I do not believe women get stripped of their identity to roam the streets."
    "This packs-of-children-in-foreign-countries-begging-for-change myth outrages me."
                "These corner immigrants need ride opportunity."

The film fails under suspicion of success.

At home, two basement mice sing 1533 Latin,

a history of steps, "musculus," "musculus"
      in the last string sonatas of Copernicus' biceps.
Launching into the sun, numbers count the possibilities
      of lines. Translated from binary, the data sings "Wish You
Were Here" in reformations large enough to fit a finger through.
      The man of gear hands, arm cranks, inflated legs,
and a saddle head rides possibilities, is locked
      to his castle. Galileo says L. natura, c. 1300 "the universe."
Though not invented yet, ten-dimension skins bump and reinvent
      through strings all possible possibilities of the possible.
A compass trick in time and space called "layer of lines"
      penciled with turning and shrinking, arrows and squiggles
maze where photons maneuver back and forth
      in three simple steps, defining movement like a clock.
Such small mechanics grace (c. 1175, L. gatia) a practical plan for heaven,
      though more readily available are toasters, TVs, and satellites
reflecting movements in perspective, mice in the gastrocnemius

since (prehistorically) Egyptians glassing and glassing
the many steps of invention, innocent
(c. 1500 BC) until Rome, the Portland vase, an Oregon
he was born to, she traveling east then west from Main,
e & w, legs weave, pump gravity for the body to swing
up to 1909 and the polymerization of phenol and formaldehyde, plastic,
an old plasticity that molds what-it-was-like into a solid, an expression
the statue wears into the ground: he's plying attention to her
in 2005 flexible stocks of glass shaped plastic must stop a bullet
though the machine behind dies out, replaced rather than repaired, older
parts of the environment museum: obsidian, Pele's tears, diamonds
give them ideas about standing and staring at a thing that does not move
for too long: history (c. 5000 BC) made history without history happening,
bones and numbers and paintings (c. 30000 BC), or dome.

Exhibit:
a tremendous crossing
of families losing family members,

letters passed on, typeset in books about send-off and diaries.
The guide was called adagio-of-the soles—

an astronomical constant in slush and dust. Many erased
at the isthmus crossing, known as the Great R.E.M. Strip,

became fisherman stories of telekinesis. The Air River Valley
survivors added whisk to their vocabulary, "not a whisk of this can leave
the room,"

"without whisk nothing will be accomplished."
Ardently agnostic, generations of their minds fevered; generations

handing their walking stick and immigration skills down,
salvitur ambulando because their lungs keep changing shape.

Newer versions
addendum place
and colloquialisms.

"Where's my donkey?"
                              or some version of this
spoke by the actor, repeated by the viewer
to put on the same cloak, be context
within an adventure with a tragic ending
                              waiting at Jiffy Lube
for an oil change, "Where's my donkey?"
in a field of wheat or rows of corn
ignoring the seeds, what makes up the seed,
and heat in the air that grows it,
                              just people standing around
feeling and talking mirror neurons
bouncing between lip twitches "Where's my donkey?"
inflected seriously, the way someone serious would do it
                              before the earth is destroyed
and powerful weapons are employed to prevent this
so the normal way of traveling can be maintained,
this cart or bus line, the driver repeating
                              to the passengers
the same stops as though for the first time.

Overhead the sound barrier opens a swimming pool

to swift attacks of vacations to come,

                              Saturdays.
               Luggage scratched with a check list:
               camera camera hat. A relaxed idea
               of "local." A fast internet connection:

Java—island crippled through binoculars,
drank mornings comfortably before prayers:
travel through the affirmative mountains, "yeah,"
off the boat, the bus, ceilings vault for which home,
deity; steam a lighter shade than the liquid
the cream dances on, the streets, the view from.

A pleasure-beach grant for the biological journal:

Whales—cetaceans (Ger. *Wale*), *n*. Boned and watered and blooded—formally known as land mammals, quickly accrued adaptations: swimming.

Hearing, therefore sound, therefore the acoustic medium seems important. Yet, how songs sing over chords without air: baffling, astonishing.

Most migration routes hug coast lines—"summer" to Homo sapiens—though from giant squid scars, as noted by Melville—1819-1891—deep diving can be postulated.

Enemies: man, *n.* Piece used in a game; also, Boned, aired, and blooded.
Enemies: some theorize intelligence.

Balaenoptera musculus reach whalehood at 5 years—though most reach faster—lack baleen—a plate collection to capture food—as babies consume 50 buttery gallons
of milk a day.

So(und) na(vigation and) r(anging)—disrupts, supposedly, underwater acoustics—known as "below the surface threat"—though deep water routes seem unaffected, which was an area of particular interest to Descartes—1596-1650—though he scrubbed himself (from the blue whale to the porpoise) clean of this allusion.

The whale's art is thought—*v.* Intention—to be its song.

[note. diagram of the spar position, head reclined, fluke resting on the shallow bottom]

When they go, they go home in flocks.

A silent oddity comes (silence), then a catch
of common words around an idea
part word, part idea, part observer
twisted together: the observer must observe this
                                        whenever it happens:
"tweet, tweet."

Field notes play like the invention of warm afternoons,
                                        many afternoons
forward along the highway at night
                        through the smell of a grandmother's cigarette
and the thick breeze of rain
                                        that puddles, dries, stains,
found in wood and wondered over: the grain
                        moves like an arm.

Note

P. 44, diagram was retrieved from the NASA website:
http://www.nasa.gov/home/

Michael Rerick lives and teaches in Portland, OR. Work recently appears or is forthcoming at *Angel City Review, Barzakh, Futures Trading, Horse Less Review, Matter, Ping Pong, Rivet Journal, Potluck Magazine, Switchback, S/Word, Tarpaulin Sky, Waccamaw,* and *Zoomoozophone.* He is also the author of *In Ways Impossible to Fold, morefrom, The Kingdom of Blizzards,* and *X-Ray.*

He a graduate from Loyola University, New Orleans (BA), University of Arizona (MFA), and University of Cincinnati (PhD). Working in the arts and community, he has also spent much time in the dish pit of many restaurants.